Hinduism

A Comprehensive Guide to the Hindu Religion, Hindu Gods, Hindu Beliefs, Hindu Rituals and Hinduism History

Table of Contents

Introduction

This book has eye-opening information about Hinduism that will help you to understand the religion, the Gods, beliefs, rituals and how it has evolved over time.

Hindus, and Hinduism: What comes to mind at the thought of these two terms? Breathtaking temples, Indians, worship of a cow, the red dot or burning incense and other rituals? With over a billion adherents, the religion is perhaps one of the least understood religions, especially among the major religions of the world (it is the third most populous religion, yet the least understood). Think about it; a religion with no specific founder, one where there is no one specific 'holy' book like in Christianity and Islam, and one with no agreed set of teachings is definitely likely to be very confusing for the average person.

I know you might be wondering:

Does Hinduism really have many Gods? Why do Hindus worship the cow? How about the dot... why do they wear it near the middle of their forehead? Why are they forbidden to eat meat...? These are just a few of the countless questions many people ask or wonder about Hinduism, and, whether you are a Hindu or not, there must be questions you may be desiring to get answers to as regards to the Hindu culture/practices, religion or even their history.

Hinduism is special and has a lot of material, perhaps because it is the oldest known religion in the world. It therefore provides a lot to learn, and you do not want to miss out on ANYTHING in our journey through Hinduism as we explore the main aspects of Hinduism including the Gods, culture, the structure of their society, beliefs and so on.

Did you know that the supreme spirit in Hinduism is believed to be both male and female? Well, you will discover more than you ever imagined exists in Hinduism and by the end of this book, you'll be well versed with a religion that has over one billion followers worldwide. Let's begin.

Because Hinduism is a strange religion for many people who do not follow the religion, it can be very difficult to understand different concepts, especially when there is use of a non-English term. To ensure you don't get lost in the process of reading this book, we will start off with a few basic details about Hinduism to put everything into context before delving deep into the main topics, but first off, you can study the glossary below lightly and refer to it accordingly as you read the book.

Getting Started: A Glossary for Beginners

Jyotish- Made of light (comes from 'jyoti' which means light and 'ish' which is the prefix of the Sanskrit word 'Ishwar/God' which means 'made of')

Karma- This refers to the sum of the actions of an individual in the current and former states of existence, which is usually considered as determining their fate in impending existences.

Vedanta- This refers to a system of Indian philosophy that literally means the end of the verdas.

Vatsu- This simply refers to a Hindu system of architecture- the texts that describe the principles of layout, design, measurements, space arrangements, ground preparation and special geometry.

Ayurveda- This refers to the traditional Hindu system of medicine that's based on the notion of balance in bodily systems and uses herbal treatment, diet and yogic breathing.

Indology- This refers to the study of Indian history, culture and philosophy.

Rama- This refers to the seventh avatar of Vishnu, the Hindu god.

The guru-shishya tradition- Also known as parampara (lineage), it denotes a succession of disciples and teachers in the traditional Indian culture and religion.

Incarnation- Incarnation refers to the rebirth doctrine in Hinduism, and also its theistic traditions to the avatar. Literally speaking, Avatar means alight, descent, to make an appearance; it also refers to the representation of the presence of a deity or a superhuman being in another form.

Bhagavata- This refers to the One devoted to God (Bhagavat).

Satguru- This is the title that's given specifically to a saint or enlightened rishi whose purpose in life is to direct the initiated shishya on the spiritual path towards realizing himself through the realization of the Omnipresent (God).

Sadhu- This refers to a sage or a holy man.

Swami- This simply means a religious teacher.

Moksha- It is the release from the rebirth cycle that's impelled by the law of karma. You can also refer to it as the transcendent state that's attained as a consequence of being released from this cycle.

Durga- This refers to the 'invisible' or 'inaccessible,' who is Devi's most popular incarnation and also one of the forms of the Goddess Shakti.

Kali- This refers to the Hindu goddess of time, death and doomsday. She's at times associated with violence and sexuality but also considered to be a strong mother-figure and a symbol of motherly-love.

Ambika- Goddess Durga's avatar.

Advaita Vedanta- Refers to a type of Hinduism. The people who believe in it believe that their souls are never different from God. Atman is the Sanskrit word for soul and Brahman is the Sanskrit word for God.

Bhakti- This refers to devotion or love for a personal god or a devotee's representational god.

Maya- The supernatural power that gods and demons have to produce illusions.

Agamas- (literally refers to 'tradition') it denotes the doctrines and precepts that have come down as tradition.

Consort- This simply refers to a counterpart of a major God or Goddess.

Ishvara- (based on the medieval Hindu texts) refers to God, Supreme being, special self or personal god.

Ardhanarishvara- This refers to a composite male and female (or androgynous) form of God Shiva and Parvati, His consort. Ardhanarishvara is typically depicted as half female and half male, split down at the center.

Sadhana- This refers to the daily spiritual practice. Sadhana is the main tool Hindus use to work on themselves to achieve life's purpose.

Avatar and avatar's doctrine- An avatar refers to the 'descent' of the divine realm of material existence for the purpose of (usually) restoring and protecting dharma- or righteousness and cosmic order. The avatar doctrine is a basically a seminal concept in particular Hinduism forms – for instance, Vaishnavism, whose followers worship Vishnu as the supreme God.

Tantra- This refers to the Hindu ritual or mystical text that dates up to the 13th century. Tantra is also the adherence to the principles of the tantras that involve yoga, mantras, yoga, rituals and meditation.

Jnana- This is a Sanskrit term referring to 'wisdom' or spiritual knowledge. This knowledge cannot be separated from the Divine (not entirely worldly).

Yantras- These are the geometrical designs that are imprinted on silver or copper plates that Hindus use to worship Deities at home or in temples or even as an aid during meditation. Many people use them for the benefits they offer by their supposed occult powers - according to the tantric texts and Hindu astrology.

Left hand and right hand tantra- practitioners usually divide Tantra into two paths (right-hand and left-hand path). The right handed tantra rites uses the Veda principles in a way that is in line with nature (in a way that supports life, creates increasing levels of coherence, health and integration of the society and individual). Thus, proper meditation is actually a right-handed tantric system that you can refer to as 'natural.'

The left-hand tantric techniques, on the other hand, are largely unnatural. The left-hand tantra is an approach that doesn't really honor the whole aspect of the system involved. It's more like using a chewing gum stick's foil wrapper to replace a fuse. Results might be realized, but at a cost, or great risk. They are a quick fix and usually create immediate and flashy results - many 'magic' tricks performed by 'spiritual teachers' in India are the outcome of right-hand tantra.

Sattva- This is the quality of truth, goodness, serenity, wholesomeness, positivity, balance, wholeness, confidence, creativity, virtuousness, constructiveness and peacefulness that is drawn towards, Jnana and dharma.

Rigveda- This literally means shine or praise and knowledge. It is an Indian collection of ancient Vedic Sanskrit hymns, and one of the four canonical sruti (sacred texts) of Hinduism called the Vedas.

Shakti Peetha or Sakti Pitha- literally refers to the seat of Shakti. Shakti Peethas are important shrines and destinations of pilgrimage on Shaktism, the Hindu tradition that is goddess-focused. We have between 52 and 108 Sakti Pithas by different accounts, of which 4 to 18 are known as Maha (or major) in the Hindu texts of the medieval period.

Samsara- This refers to the death and rebirth cycle which life in the material world is bound to.

Sanskrit: This is the main/primary (ancient) language used in Hinduism. It was the language used as a means of dialogue/communication by the Hindu celestial Gods and the Indo-Aryans of the time.

Now that you have a basic understanding of different terms used in Hinduism, you are now set to start learning about this great religion. Let's start from the beginning.

Hinduism: A Comprehensive Background
A Quick Summary

What is Hinduism?

Hinduism is the world's third largest religion based on the number of followers, with over 1 billion followers, after Christianity and Islam. It is the main religion in India and Nepal.

The term Hinduism is obtained from a Sanskrit word, which when translated simply means "the dwellers by the Indus River." It is one of the oldest known religions, with sacred writing dating as far back as 1400-1500 BC. And it is an interesting and complex one, too, with millions of gods (an estimated 330 million of them!), unlike many other religions that have few gods. But even with the many gods, Hinduism also has a supreme god known as Brahma, an entity that is believed to inhabit every bit of reality and existence throughout the universe. Brahma is both unknowable and impersonal and is believed to exist in 3 distinct forms, namely Shiva, the destroyer, Vishnu, the preserver, and Brahma, the creator.

Another interesting feature about the religion is that it has no single founder, set of agreed teachings, or a single scripture. Instead, it has its main texts in the form of Vedas, Ramayana, Sutras, Aranyakas, Brahmanas, Mahabharata and Upanishadas, which contain stories, poems, rituals, philosophies, incantations and hymns from which various sects base their beliefs.

Well, the truth is, it is impossible to summarize Hinduism given that various Hindu schools have numerous elements of almost every theological system. Depending on how you look at it, Hinduism can be:

- Monistic: whereby only one thing exists - the Sankara's school
- Panentheistic: Whereby the world is part of God - the Ramanuja's school
- Pantheistic: Whereby one divine thing exists to make sure God is identical to the world - the Brahmanism.
- Theistic: Whereby only one God who is distinct from the creation exists- Bhakti Hinduism.

With that quick summary of the religion, let's delve a little further into the details.

Basic Facts: Digging Deep

As you have seen, I have labelled Hinduism as a religion, and many people, including scholars, tend to look at it as a religion. Nonetheless, if you look at it more critically, you'll find that it is actually more than that; it is essentially a large and complex socio-religious body that in a way reflects the intricacy of the Indian society. Look at it this way: Different creeds, many languages and dialects, and a rich geography, among other elements, have molded Hinduism and made it extremely heterogenic. We don't have a unifying overall religious authority or some book claiming supreme truth or dogmas, and that has actually taken a role in the diversity of Hinduism too. According to me, it is fair to say that even the texts we find in Hinduism claiming to have some divine inspiration don't declare themselves as being better than any other and try to co-exist in a tolerant manner.

The numerous manifestations of Hinduism go from highly intellectual philosophies that concern many and puzzling metaphysical concerns, mental and physical exercises such as yoga, rituals to simple legends and tales.

The Hindus cover about a seventh of the world's population and its origins are in the vast Indian subcontinent. Even though it remains the majority Indian religion, with more than 800 million adherents, its cultural, spiritual, linguistic and social influences extend across the globe since today, there are over 60 million Hindus living in 150 different countries outside India, including the UK with about 700,000 and North America with more than 2 million.

Before we discuss more about it, you should, however, note that Hinduism is not monolithic - where it is characterized or categorized by complete uniformity - and this is a reason why it has eluded a simple definition. It also doesn't have a single founder, no single set of teachings, no single scripture, no central governing body and certainly, no unified code of conduct. This is the reason why it was perplexing for early scholars of religion because they had a tendency to perceive Hinduism through their individual preconceived thoughts of the nature of religion, which was most often relative to their own faith and culture.

Hinduism is, in fact, a family of numerous diverse sampradayas, or traditions, each of which contains its own distinct theology, rituals, philosophy, value system and code of practices. This is an inescapable richness and diversity that makes Hinduism interesting to study, but also hard to define in precise and simple terms. However, just like in a typical family, we have common elements and unifying themes in Hinduism which include accepting a supreme Reality or God, dharma (the law of righteousness), atman (the soul), moksha (liberation), karma (the law of cause and effect, and the authority of the Vedas (most ancient Hindu scriptures). We'll discuss these and what they mean in the course of this book.

As you probably know, Hinduism is responsible for numerous contributions to the world, such as that of the practice and concepts of karma, Yoga, Jyotish, Vatsu, Ayurveda, Vedanta and so many more.

Although it is difficult to define Hinduism, we can certainly say that it's closely related to India, its sacred texts and culture, and also extends far beyond them.

Then you might wonder: How did such a complex, almost impossible to define, religion start? How has it evolved over time? That's what we will discuss next.

A Journey through Time: The History of Hinduism

First and foremost, you have to appreciate that the early history of Hinduism is difficult to date with certainty, but we generally have a rough chronology that largely gives us the history. In this section, we'll talk briefly about the following periods to guide us through:

- The Indus Valley Civilization (Before 2000 BCE)
- The Vedic Period (1500–500 BCE)
- The Epic, Puranic as well as Classical Age (500 BCE–500 CE)
- Medieval Period (500 CE–1500 CE)
- Pre-Modern Period (1500–1757 CE)
- British Period (1757–1947 CE)
- Independent India (1947 CE–the present)

The Indus Valley Civilization

The Indus valley civilization was situated in the basin of river Indus that passes through the present-day Pakistan. It had developed by about 2500 BCE, even though its origins date back to the Neolithic period.

The Indus Valley was similar to the civilizations of Mesopotamia. The civilization was very extensive - from the foothills of the Himalayas in the east to the Lothar on the coast of Gujarat, and to the Iranian border (Sutgagen Dor).

In the Indus Valley, religion seemed to have entailed different temple rituals as well as ritual bathing in Mohenjo-Daro's 'great bath.' There is a good amount of evidence that shows that there might have been animal sacrifice at kalibangan. Some terracotta figurines have also been found, goddess images and a seal that depicts a seated figure that's surrounded by animals, which experts believed to be a prototype of the god Shiva.

It is suggested that there may be links between the Indus Valley civilization and the later Hinduism and those supporting this idea point to the ritual bathing, goddess worship and ritual bathing and sacrifice.

The Vedic Period

We have generally had two major theories talking about the early growth of the south Asian traditions, the Aryan migration thesis and the cultural transformation thesis.

The Aryan migration thesis:

States that the Indus valley groups who referred to themselves as 'Aryans,' or noble ones, migrated into the sub-continent, becoming the dominant cultural force. On this view, Hinduism stems from their religion that was recorded in the Veda together with the elements of the indigenous traditions that they found.

The cultural transformation thesis:

It states that the Aryan culture is a development of the culture of the Indus Valley. It states that there weren't any Aryan migrations or invasions and the culture of the Indus Valley was a Vedic or Aryan culture.

We also have archaeology and language being two important sources of knowledge about this ancient period. Let me briefly say something about that.

The Vedic culture spoke a language known as Vedic Sanskrit. Sanskrit is linked to other languages contained in the Indo-European language group and this would mean that the Indo-European speakers shared a linguistic origin usually referred to as Proto-Indo-European.

There, however, lacks a clear archaeological connection in the Indian subcontinent starting from the Neolithic period, making the history of the period complicated. For instance, there has been a debate about there being no horse remains found in the Indus Valley, even though horse sacrifice is central in the Veda.

The Vedic religion

There are some Vedic rituals which were largely elaborate and still continue to date. Sacrifice was offered to the various devas or gods living in various realms of a universe made up of hierarchies, and categorized into 3 broad realms: the sky, earth and atmosphere.

The earth has the fire god known as Agni, the plant god known as Soma and the priestly power god known as Brhaspati.

The atmosphere has the warrior known as Indra, the storm gods Maruts and Rudra and the wind known as Vayu.

The sky, on the other hand, has Dyaus, the sky god who's from the same root as Zeus, the Lord of cosmic law or 'rta' known as Varuna, his friend Mirta, the god of night, the pervader known as Vishnu and Pushan, the nourisher.

Epic, Puranic and Classical Age

This is the period that saw the composition of more texts, the Shastras, Dharma Sutras, the two epics known as Ramayana and Mahabharata, and subsequently, the Puranas which contained many of the stories that are still very popular today. The Bhagavad Gita is part and parcel of the Mahabharata.

The idea of dharma, or law, duty and truth (which is very fundamental to Hinduism) was expressed in some texts known as Shastras and Dharma Sutras. The Dharma Sutras recognize the three dharma sources which include the tradition (smrti), revelation (that is the Veda) and good custom.

The Vedic fire sacrifice became minimized during this period as the devotional worship developed and images of deities in temples. As the Gupta Empire rose, the period saw the growth of the great Vaishnavism traditions, Shaktism (which focused on Devi) and Shaivism (which focused on Shiva).

Since this period, we are able to recognize numerous elements in the present-day Hinduism like the bhakti (that refers to devotion) and temple worship. Poetic literature also developed during this period. These texts were first written in Sanskrit which then became the most significant element in a culture that was shared.

Medieval Period

Since 500 CE, there has been a rise of devotion to the major deities and especially Devi, Vishnu and Shiva. The Gupta Empire collapsed and regional kingdoms developed and began patronizing different religions. For instance, the Cholas residing in the South supported Shaivism.

In this period, there was the development of Jagganaha in Puri, the Shiva temple in Tanjvur, Tamilnadu and Cidambaram, among other great regional temples. All these temples installed a major deity and even became centers of political and religious power.

The poet-saints and gurus

During this time, there was a development of religious literature written in Sanskrit and also in different vernacular languages, and mainly Tamil. The poet-saints usually recorded their devotional sentiments here and the most remarkable include the 12 Vaishnava Alvars (6th-7th centuries) which include a prominent female poet-saint known as Andal, and the 63 Shaiva Nayanars (8th -10th centuries).

The later teachers and key thinkers (gurus or acharyas) started consolidating these teachings. They came up with new theologies, preserved by their own disciplic successions or sampradaya.

A famous guru is Shankara (780-820) who travelled widely and defeated scholars of the unorthodox movements which had established prominent seats of learning through India about the turn of the millennium. He restored the establishment of the Vedic canon authority and propagated monism (advaita) before laying foundations for more development of the tradition referred to as the Vedanta.

Pre-Modern Period

There was the rise of Islam in the North together with the development of the Hindu traditions that were most widespread in the South. It became a religious and political force in India. Islam managed to reach the Indian shores about the 8th century through traders who were plying the Arabian Sea and the Muslim armies that had captured the provinces in the Northwest.

With the Turkish Sultanate (around 12oo CE), Muslim political power began and thus arose the Mughul empire (starting from 1526). There was a liberal emperor known as Akbar (1542-1605) who allowed Hindus to practice freely. Nonetheless,

Aurangzeb (1618-1707), his great grandson, restricted Hindu practice and destroyed many of their temples.

This period saw more developments in the devotional religion, or bhakti. The northern-based Sant tradition (mainly in the Punjab and Maharashtra) did express devotion in poetry to nirguna, a god with no qualities, and saguna, a god with qualities; for instance, parental love of his followers.

The Sant tradition blends some features of bhakti, yoga or meditation and Islamic mysticism. Even today, princess Mirabai's poetry and those of the other saints, including Surdas, Tukaram and Dadu, remain very popular.

British Period

In 1757, there was a battle in India known as the battle of Plassey in which Robert Clive won. Well, that battle brought an end to the Mughul Empire and, subsequently, the rise of the British Reign in India.

At first, the British did not attempt to interfere with the culture and religion of the Indian people. They allowed them to practice their religion unconstrained. However, things changed later when the missionaries arrived at their shores preaching Christianity. The first scholars arrived and, even though sympathetic at first, were often driven by a desire to westernize the local people. Nonetheless, Indology chairs were established in Oxford, among other universities across Europe. Years later, an age of reformation would come about in India.

The Hindu Reformers

There developed a Hindu Renaissance in the 19th century during which reformers like Ram Mohan Roy (1772-1833) depicted Hinduism as a rational and ethical religion, and went ahead to build the Brahmo Samaj (a Hindu reform movement) to further these ideas.

There was another reformer, Dayananda Sarasvati (1824-83), who advocated for the reinstating of the Vedic religion that emphasized an eternal impersonal and omnipotent God. He sought the return to the sanatana dharma, or the eternal law of Hinduism, earlier than the Puranas and the Epics through the Arya Samaj, his society.

These two reformers wanted to rid Hinduism of what they saw as superstition and thus became part of the groups that were really instrumental in sowing the seeds of the nationalism of India and also the Hindu missionary movements, which later travelled to the west.

There was another important figure you should note, Paramahamsa Ramakrishna (1836-86). He promoted the unity of all religions and his ideas were developed by Vivekananda (1863-1902), his disciple. Vivekananda linked these ideas to a political vision of a united India.

These are the ideas that were later developed by Gandhi (1849-1948) who is known for being a key contributor in the creation of an independent India.

Mahatma Gandhi, who was both a politician and holy man, could be the most famous Indian of the 20th century. He assisted in negotiating independence but was extremely disappointed when his country was partitioned. In 1948, he was assassinated.

A lot of the strength and conviction of Gandhi was drawn from the Hindu teachings, such as the principle of non-violence (ahimsa), and he put forward a patriotism that was noble and broad-minded.

Hindutva

As the Indians went on resisting the colonial rule, the word 'Hindu' became charged with political and cultural meaning. A central idea was 'hindu-ness' or 'hindutva' that was coined by VD Savarkar to refer to a socio-political force, which could actually bring together the Hindus against being aggressive to others.

This ideal has been embraced and developed by cultural organizations such as the Vishva Hindu Parishad (VHP) and Rashtriya Svayam-Sevak Sangh (RSS) and received political expression in the Bharatiya Janata Party (BJP). These sectarian ideas went on after independence.

Independent India

When India was partitioned in 1947, the bloodshed that resulted strengthened nationalistic tendencies and particularly the notations of Hinduism as an Indian religion and India as a 'Hindu country.' These tendencies have endured and, since then, there has been a frequent eruption of communal violence. Hindus were incited to destroy the Babri Mosque in Ayodhya in 1992, which they were made to believe was built provocatively and deliberately over Rama's birth site. There have also been attempts to convert Hindus to other religions, and this has exacerbated tension and become even worse when combined with the reactions by the Hindutva movement.

The Hindu Diaspora

The post-war Hindu movements, however, imported into the west, and the increased migration of Hindus led to the rise of many questions about the nature of the Hindu identity. Since the 1960s, there were many Indians migrating to North America and Britain. Gurus journeyed to the west to nurture the fledgling, or green, Hindu communities and would at times begin missionary movements, which managed to attract western interest.

For instance, Transcendental meditation achieved international popularity in the late 1960s and attracted the attention of celebrities like the Beatles. I'm sure you have heard about the Hare Krishna movement, which became one of the most conspicuous. This movement is identified by male followers who sport saffron robes and shaved heads.

Many of these western adherents and casual yoga practitioners were also attracted to the spiritual aspects of Hinduism.

At the close of the millennium, different Hindu communities around the world became a bit more established overseas and excelled socially, academically and economically. They built many great temples, like the famous Swaminarayan Temple based in London.

Hindus in the diaspora became particularly more concerned about the preservation of their tradition and religion. Consequently, they felt it necessary to respond to the Hindu youth who wanted to have a rational understanding of the essence of the different practices that were being passed down through families. At the moment, they are particularly concerned about the best way to deal with issues that are pretty contentious, like intermarriage, caste, and the position of the woman. In more ways than one, Hindus in the west are going back to their roots.

If you thought the short history of Hinduism is complicated, you should know that for more than 200 years, scholars have had a hard time understanding Hinduism itself; a faith which had its followers worshipping one of the many Gods as the supreme, the religion that is massively diverse in its practices, beliefs and methods of worship. There are some Indologists who labeled the Hinduism they came across as polytheistic (which many still think to be the case today) and even came up with new terms such as henotheism to describe this mysterious display of spiritual traditions. There are, however, a few who have realized, and even fewer who have written, that the "eternal faith," or Sanatana Dharma, of India that's widely known today as Hinduism is made up of many followers worldwide and is a group of religions with four main denominations: Smartism, Shaktism, Savism and Vaishnavism. You will realize that this single perception is important for understanding Hinduism better and accurately explaining it to other people.

Let's talk about these denominations in brief.

The four Hindu Denominations

Contrary to the current misconceptions, the Hindu people worship one Supreme being, but use different names.

- For the Vaishnavites, the God is Lord Vishnu.
- For the Saivites, the God is Siva.
- For the Shaktkas, the Goddess Shakti remains supreme.
- The Smartas are known as the liberal Hindus and it is up to the individual devotee to decide their Deity.

Each one of them has a multitude of guru lineages, priesthoods, religious leaders, sacred literature, schools, monastic communities, uncountable temples, and pilgrimage centers. They have a lot of wealth of architecture and art, scholarship and philosophy. The four sects contain extremely divergent beliefs that each one has become a full religion that is also independent. Even so, they share a great cultural heritage, dharma, karma belief, reincarnation, temple worship, guru-shishya tradition, all-pervasive Divinity, manifold Deities, sacraments and the scriptural authority known as the Vedas.

NOTE: Each one of the philosophies, lineages and schools of Hinduism share a common purpose, which is to further the unfoldment of the soul to its divine destiny. This process is not presented anywhere better than in the development of the famous lotus which arises from the mud, seeking the sun, to become a magnificent flower. Its blossom, as the gurus say, is a promise of perfection and purity.

Let's discuss in more detail the denominations themselves (including a concise comparison).

Denominations in Hinduism

Saivism

The Saivite Hindus worship the Hindu Supreme God as Siva, who is known as the compassionate one. The Saivites greatly regard philosophy and self-discipline and follow a satguru. They practice yoga and worship in the temple. They always strive to be one with Siva within.

Saivism is also regarded as the world's oldest religion and stresses the guru's centrality and a type of yoga, known as bhakti-raja-siddha, that leads to oneness with Siva, within.

The sacred Himalayan abode of Lord Siva, called Mount Kailas, is known to embody the pinnacle of consciousness.

As it is ancient, Saivism is ageless - it doesn't have a beginning. It is the originator of the multi-faceted religion that we now call Hinduism, and scholars have managed to trace the roots of Siva to over 8,000 years to the Indus Valley Civilization, which was pretty advanced going by the standards of those days - but the sacred writings offer a conflicting view, asserting that there was really never a time when Saivism didn't exist.

History as we know it today records six key schools in this denomination, which include Kashmir Saivism, Siddha Siddhanta, Saiva Siddhanta, Pashupatism, Vira Saivism and Siva Advaita. The grandeur and beauty of Saivism exists in a practical culture, a view of the place of man in the universe and a deep system of temple spirituality/mysticism and siddha yoga. It is also known to give knowledge of the evolution of man from God and back to God, of the unfoldment of the soul and awakening, though guided by the enlightened sages.

Just like all the sects, the majority of Savites are devout families headed by many orders of sadhus and Swamis following the very strict path (which renounces worldly pleasures) to moksha." The Vedas state:

"When you know Siva, the Auspicious one who's hidden in everything, surpassingly fine, like film rising from butter, the One embracer of the universe by realizing God, one is released from all fetters," Aum Namah Sivaya

16

Shaktism

The Shaktas worship the Supreme as the Shakti, the Divine Mother or Devi. She definitely has many forms, some of which are fierce and others gentle. The Shaktas use real magic, chants, yoga, rituals and holy diagrams to summon cosmic forces and rouse from the spine, the great kundalini power.

Shakti radiates beauty, compassion, energy and protection for her followers- she is depicted in a green form. She dons the Shakta sect's tilaka on her forehead and is known to bless her devotees, who "hold an umbrella, shower rosewater and prostrate her feet."

The worship of Shakti goes beyond the pale history, and, even so, Shakta Hinduism originated from an organized Indian sect about the 5th century. Currently, it contains four expressions: devotional, yogic, folk-shamanic and universalist - all summoning the fierce power of Durga or Kali, or the 'benign grace' of Ambika or Parvati.

- The devotionists of Shakti use puja rites (particularly to the Shri Chakra yantra) to build intimacy with the Goddess.
- Shamanic Shaktism uses magic, fire-walking, trance mediumship and animal sacrifice for prophecy, healing, and fertility, and the yogis seek to invoke the sleeping Goddess Kundalini to join her with Siva in the sahasrara chakra.
- The Shakta Universalists follow the transformed Vendantic tradition that is demonstrated by Sri Ramakrishna. The 'left hand' tantric rites go beyond the traditional codes of ethics. The left hand here denotes the practice of worshiping the chakras (chakra puja). Chakra refers to the center of consciousness in your body.

Since Shaktisim is mainly advaitic, it defines the destiny of the soul as complete identity with the Unmanifest, Siva. The Central scriptures include the Vedas, Puranas and Shakta Agamas.

"We bow down to the universal soul of all. Above and below and in all four directions, Mother of the universe, we bow." Aum Chandikayai Namah.

Vaishnavism

The Vaishnavites worship and adulate the Supreme as Lord Vishnu and His incarnations, which include Rama and Krishna. The Vaishnavites are mostly dualistic. They are profoundly devotional and their religion has many saints, scriptures and temples.

Vishnu is believed to be the infinite ocean, which the world emerges from. He stands on waves, encircled by Seshanaga (who has many heads), who embodies agelessness and is esteemed as an important extension of divine energy and Balarama's incarnation, the brother of Lord Krishna.

The worship of Vishnu dates back to the Vedic times. The Bhagavata sects were very popular before 300 BCE. The five Vaishnava schools we have today were started in the middle ages by Madhva, Ramanuja, Chaitanya, Vallabha and Nimbarka. Vaishnaism stresses single-pointed surrender to Vishnu, prapatti or his incarnations which are ten or so, known as avatars.

Festivals and temple worship are observed elaborately and philosophically in this denomination.

God and Soul are eternally distinct – the destiny of the soul is to worship God eternally and enjoy him, through his grace. Vaishnavism has a very strong monastic community even though it's generally nonascetic, encouraging bhakti as the highest path. The central scriptures that are used here are the Vedas, Puranas, Vaishnava Agamas and Itihasas.

"On those who meditate on Me and worship with undivided heart, I confer attainment of what they have not, and preserve what they have." Aum Namo Narayanaya.

Smartism

The Smartas worship the supreme in any of the following forms: Vishnu, Sakti, Ganesha, Skanda and Siva. They are usually referred to as non-sectarian or liberal because they accept all the major Gods in Hinduism. They follow a meditative and philosophical path and emphasize man's oneness with God through understanding.

Adi Sankara, who lived for only 32 years (788-820 CE), was the one who gave Hinduism the new liberal denomination called Smartism. He is depicted as wearing sacred marks, holding his writings and flanked by six Deities of the Smarta altar who include Siva, Shakti, Surya the Sun, Vishnu, Ganesha and Kumaran.

Smarta essentially means a follower of the classical smriti, and especially the Puranas, Dharma Shatras and Itihasas. The Smartas honor the Agamas and revere the Vedas. This faith is currently synonymous with the teachings of the monk-philosopher Adi Sankara, who is also referred to as shanmata sthapanacharya (meaning the founder of the system made up of six sects). Sankara made campaigns throughout India to consolidate the Hindu faiths that existed in his time under the 'Advaita Vedanta' banner. He also propagated the ancient Smarta altar of five Dietiesb- Ganapati, Siva, Shakti, Surya and Vishnu - and then added Kumara. The devotees could therefore select their preferred Deity from these.

Sankara also organized hundreds of monasteries into a ten-order dashanami system that now contains five pontifical centers. He wrote copious commentaries on the Brahma Sutras, Upanishads and Bhagavad Gita. Sankara himself proclaimed:

"It is the one Reality which appears to our ignorance as a manifold universe of names and forms and changes. Like the gold of which many ornaments are made, it remains in itself unchanged. Such is Brahman, and That art Thou." Aum Namah Sivaya.

As you have seen, the entire spectrum of Hindu religiousness is located within four main denominations, or sects, mentioned above. Among the four streams, there certainly are similarities and differences, with the former taking the larger proportion. Before we start comparing them in the next subsection, there are a few preliminary points I would like to make:

All four believe in reincarnation and karma, and also in a supreme being who is both form and pervades form, and also who creates the universe, sustains it and destroys it only to create it again in endless cycles. The four believe in maya - 'magic' or 'illusion' (even though their definitions differ a bit on this one) - and also in the liberation of the soul right from rebirth, known as moksha, as the ultimate goal or end of human existence.

Moreover, they declare rather strongly the validity and significance of temple worship and the many Gods and devas in the three worlds of existence that they believe in.

They also seem to agree that there is no intrinsic evil and also that the universe is created out of God, and it is He who permeates it.

They all believe in dharma and in non-injury, 'ahimsa,' and also in the essence/importance of a satguru in leading the soul toward Self Realization.

They wear tilaka, sacred marks on their foreheads, as sacred symbols, even though each one wears a somewhat distinct mark. Lastly, they prefer cremation of their bodies when they die and believe that the soul will occupy another body in the next life.

While Hinduism contains many sacred scriptures, all its sects assign the highest authority to the Agamas and Vedas, even though their Agamas differ a bit. Let's now look at a short comparison of these denominations, based on the following parameters:

A Comparison of The Different Denominations

1. On the Goddess or Personal God

Saivism- The temple Deity and personal God is Siva, who is not a male or female. Lord Karttikeya and Lord Ganesha are also worshipped.

Shaktism- The temple Deity and personal Goddess is Shakti, or Shri Devi, who is a female. She is worshipped as Parvati, Amman, Rajarajeshvari, Kali, Divine mother, Sarasvati or Lakshmi.

Vaishnavism- The temple Deity and personal God is Ishvara, who is male. His incarnations are Krishna and Rama, and are also worshipped, along with Radharani, his divine consort.

Smartism- The temple Deity and personal God is Ishvara, who can take the form of a male or female. He/she is worshipped as Vishnu, Shakti, Siva, Surya and Ganesha or any Deity (as the devotee chooses), for instance, Krishna or Kumara.

2. On Shakti's nature

Savism- Shakti is the inseparable power of God Shiva and is known to manifest energy.

Shatism- Shakti is an immanent Being that is active, separate from the gentle (quiescent) and remote Siva.

Vaishnavism- Shakti is not given any special importance. Nonetheless, there are parallels in which the divine consorts are conceived as Vishnu's inseparable powers (and those of his incarnations too - for instance; Rama's Sita and Krishna's Radharani).

Smartism- Shakti is seen as the divine form of Ishvara, God's manifesting power.

3. On Personal God's nature

Saivism- God Siva is compassion, pure love, immanent, transcendent and normally pleased with the purity and sadhana of his followers.

Shaktism- Goddess Shakti is terrifying and compassionate at the same time, wrathful, pleasing and assuaged by the submission and sacrifice of his people.

Vaishnavism- God Vishnu is both loving and beautiful, and is the object of the devotion of man, happy by the surrender and service of his followers.

Smartism- Ishvara usually appears like a human Deity - based on the loving worship of the devotee, which is at times considered a rudimentary and self-purifying practice.

4. On Avatara's Doctrine

Saivism- the Supreme Being doesn't have any divine earthly incarnations.

Shaktism- The divine mother incarnates on this earth.

Vaishnavism- Vishnu has about ten incarnations.

Smartism- All the Deities can take up earthly incarnations.

5. On God and the Soul

Saivism- God Siva is united with the soul and the soul has to realize this advaitic or monistic Truth by the grace of God Siva.

Shaktism-Shakti, the Divine Mother is a mediatrix (mediator) - she bestows advaitic moksha on the people who worship Her.

Vaishnavism- The soul and God are completely distinct. The destiny of the Soul is to worship God and enjoy him.

Smartism- Man and Ishvara are essentially absolute Brahman. The soul and Ishvara appear dualistic (as two) within maya.

6. Spiritual Practice

Saivism- The emphasis is placed on tapas (austerity), sadhana and yoga, with bhakti as a base.

Shaktism- The emphasis is on tantra, bhakti and, from time to time, occult.

Vaishnavism- The emphasis is on the surrender or supreme bhakti known as prapatti. It's generally non-ascetic and devotional.

Smartism- The preparatory sadhanas include yoga, bhakti, raja and karma. Here, the highest path is via knowledge, which leads to jnana.

7. Key Scriptures

Saivism- Saiva Agamas, Vedas and Saiva Puranas.

Shaktism- Shakta Agamas or Tantras, Vedas and Puranas.

Vaishnavism- Vaishnava Agamas, Vedas, the Itihasas (Mahabharata and Ramayana, particularly the Bhagavad Gita) and Puranas.

Smartism- Vedas, Itihasas, Agamas and the classical smriti Puranas, particularly the Bhagavad Gita, among others.

8. Regions of Influence

Saivism- It's very widespread, strongest in North and South India, Sri Lanka and Nepal.

Shaktism- It's very widespread, but most popular in Northeast India, mainly Bengal and Assam.

Vaishnavism- Also very widespread, and strong throughout India (North and South).

Smartism- It's very widespread, but most prominent in South and North India.

9. Paths of Attainment

Saivism- The savite path is categorized into four stages of practice and belief, known as jnana, yoga, kriya and charya. The soul evolves through reincarnation and karma from the instinctive intellectual sphere into moral and virtuous living, and then into devotion and temple worship. These stages are followed by yoga or internalized worship, and the meditative disciplines it carries. It is believed that being one with God Siva is attained through the grace of the satguru and culminates in the maturity of the soul in the state of wisdom or jnana. Saivism values yoga and bhakti, contemplative and devotional sadhanas/disciplines.

Shaktism- Shaktism contains spiritual practices that are largely similar to those in Saivism, but Shaktism puts more emphasis on the power of God as opposed to mantras, Being and yantras, and also on accepting the apparent opposites (which include absolute-relative, male-female, cause-effect, pleasure-pain and mind-body). There are particular sects within Shaktism that carry out the 'left-hand' tantric rites and consciously use the world of form to change and in the end, transcend that world. Experts point out that the 'left-hand' approach is quite occult in nature and is considered 'narrow,' or a path for the few. We have the 'right-hand' that is more conservative in nature (see glossary).

Vaishnavism: According to most vaishnavites, religion is the performance of devotional disciplines and bhakti sadhanas, and that man can communicate with and get the grace of the Goddesses and Gods through the sight (or darshan) of their icons. The karma yoga and jnana yoga paths lead to bhakti yoga. One of the main practices of vaishnavites is chanting the Avataras' holy names and Vishnu's incarnations, especially Krishna and Rama. Liberation from the cycle of reincarnation (samsara) is attained through complete self-surrender to Krishna or his consort Radharani and to Vishnu.

Smartism: The Smartas, who are regarded as the most eclectic of the Hindus, hold the belief that they can only achieve moksha through yoga or jnana alone - defined as a meditative and intellectual but non-kundalini yoga path. The progressive stages of Jnana yoga are scriptural study (shravana), sustained meditation (dhyana) and reflection (manana). As an initiate, you meditate on yourself as Brahman, the Absolute reality, in order to break through maya's (see glossary) illusion - this is, however, with the guidance of a guru as you are 'affirmed to the unreality of the world.' As a devotee, you may also choose from either of some three other non-successive paths to accumulate some good karma, cultivate devotion and purify the mind. These include raja yoga, karma yoga and bhakti yoga, which particular Smartas teach that can also bring forth enlightenment.

Those are the features of the four denominations of Hinduism. As you noticed, I mentioned most of the Gods and Goddesses of Hinduism - but there is more than just what we've highlighted about them. I will dedicate this next chapter for an overview of the Hindu Deities and avatars so that you have a deeper understanding of them, and the Hindu religion as a whole.

The Hindu Gods & Goddesses

The Hindu Gods and Goddesses belong to a large family of gods that are headed by Para Shakti/ Mother Goddess as His independent or dependent aspect on one side or Supreme Brahman as Isvara or Purusha on the other. The pantheon of goddesses and gods went through numerous changes over time (deletions and additions) and, as a result, more complexity came about in Hindu religion. The Vedic Gods in the early Vedic period occupied a prominent place with Indra, Agni, Soma, Vayu, Adityas, Varuna, Visvadevas, Maruts, Prajapati, Brahma, Asvins, Pusans and many more playing a key role in the sacrificial rituals.

The Brahmanas, Vaisyas, Kshatriya, who formed the first Vedic society divisions worshipped their own classes of gods. When the Brahmanas sacrificed for themselves, they made offerings to their gods; when they officiated for the sacrifices where the Vaisyas and Kshatriyas were hosts or patrons of the sacrifices (yajamanas), they offered them to the gods worshipped by their patrons.

The Kshatriyas worshipped the gods of Kshatra power. They include: Soma, Indra, Rudra, Isana, Yama, Parjanya and Varuna. The Brahmanas worshipped gods such as Surya and Agni, who are of Sattvic nature, and later, Adityas.

The Vaisyas worshipped the gods of commonality, including Rudras, Vasus, Maruts and Visvadevas.

The sudras, on the other hand, worshipped Aditya, Pusan and a number of local deities, some of whom are not within the pale of Vedic tradition.

As the Kshatriya clans declined (perhaps due to internal squabbles and wars), the worship of their different gods started declining and were soon replaced by various deities well worshipped by new rulers, such as Kushanas, Nandas, Kanvas, Sakas, Barashivas and Pahlavas. These rules come from different caste and diverse social backgrounds, and worshipped a wide array of gods with some being very little known to the early Vedic people and who were never cited in the early Vedic literature.

Currently, we have numerous gods and goddesses in Hinduism and even though some people say they are hundreds and thousands, the Hindus worship mainly a few gods, who include Vishnu, Siva, Brahma, Lakshmi, Sarasvathi, Parvathi, their incarnations, manifestations and emanations.

NOTE:

Like I mentioned earlier, Hinduism is not polytheistic, even though Hindus worship many gods and goddesses; as a religion, Hinduism has elements of both polytheism and monotheism, and sometimes kathenotheism (henotheism), which is the belief in single gods where each one of them in turn stands out as the highest.

The highest God

This is illustrated pretty well in Brihadaranyaka Upanishad (3:9) - in the conversation between Vidagdha Sakalya and Yajnavalkya. In this section, Sakalya asks how many gods Hinduism has and in response, Yajnavalkya starts the conversation by saying, *"As many as mentioned in the offerings made the gods of the universe, namely three hundred and three, three thousand and three."* Sakalya however keeps on asking the same question and each time, Yajnavalkya keeps reducing the number - first to thirty-three, then six, three, two, one and half, then finally to one. He is then asked who is the one, to which he replies that he is the immortal self or person who's in the body. This means that in Hinduism, the idea or concept of a single God manifesting as many or acting as many dates back to the early Vedic period. This one God is the sum total of everything in the universe.

The highest God in Hinduism is called Brahman and is extolled as the Supreme Universal Self in the Vedas. He is both an 'unmanifested' and manifested, Non-Being and Being, non-existence (asat) and Existence (sat).

When you look at Paingala Upanishad (an early Sanskrit text), you will find His reflection in the quality of sattva being considered Ishvara, in tamas Viraj and Rajas Hiranyagarbha; the three aspects: Viraj, Ishvara and Hiranyagarbha are also identified with Siva, Vishnu and Brahma respectively. Viraj is also often described as Death (in early Upanishads like Chandogya) "for whom the whole creation is food."

Each one of the many gods and goddesses are the ears, hands, eyes and feet or Brahman alone. They represent diversity and his many dharmas or duties - only in their unified and highest aspect do they represent Brahman, the highest, or supreme Self.

I hope you now understand why Hinduism is neither polytheistic nor monotheistic (why it represents elements of both). Let's now look at a brief description of the main Hindu gods and goddesses.

The Gods Atman and Brahman

Brahman and Atman are representatives of the two eternal realities that have ever been present in existence. Actually, many schools of Hinduism today have always had the subject matter of most of their discussions being about the relationship of the two. Let me describe them in brief.

Brahman

To reiterate myself, Brahman is the premier, or highest, God. He is the absolute universal Self. He is eternal, infinite and indestructible, and in the Vedas, He is further described as both Being and non-Being, manifested and unmanifested. He contains many aspects, and in the early Vedic descriptions, you will find Him being symbolized as the Sun. In Hinduism, it is well known that those who achieve liberation get into His world and become immortal by Uttarayana, or the northern path. Brahman is, however, not worshipped in public places or in temples - He is only worshipped internally.

Atman

Hindus know Atman as the individual Self - the lord of the body (or microcosm). The Upanishads describe him as the transcendental, imperishable Self, immortal who you cannot reach through the mind or senses, but only in a state of self-absorption that is 'non-dual.' Atman, just like Brahman, is not worshipped in public areas or temples. He is worshipped internally through meditation and concentration.

The Premier Gods of Hinduism

Vishnu, Shiva and Brahman are the highest gods of Hinduism, but they don't form part of the early Vedic pantheon. It is during the southern and eastern expansion (in the Indian subcontinent) of the Vedic religion that they subsequently ascended to prominence. Let me describe these famous deities for you in brief.

Brahma

Brahma, originally known as Prajapati, is the creator god. He is the father of the gods, demons and humans; he is the first born. He is a teacher; He taught all the aforementioned about the importance of virtue and the nature of Self. He is the revealer of the Vedas to humans. He is also said to have a number of mind born sons.

The early Upanishads, as well as Vedic Hymns, credit him with incarnations and describe him as the Cosmic Person i.e. Purusha or Viraj, Hiranyagarbha and Ishvara. Some verses also describe him as Nature (Prakriti).

In the ancient times, Brahma enjoyed a highly exalted position - during the times when the very first Kshatriyas were ruling the land. When they declined, his popularity declined too. Currently, he is worshipped in a few temples only, and especially in those located in the regions forming part of the ancient Sindhu Saraswathi region or adjoining to it, where the Kshatriyas were ruling in the ancient times. Brahmaloka is known to be his abode.

Vishnu

Vishnu is presently the most popular Hindu god and currently, Vaishnavism is the most dominant and popular Hindu sect that has a number of subsects and autonomous teacher traditions. The Vishnu devotees worship Him as the Supreme Brahman who is the highest. He is also considered (in popular Hinduism) the preserver, who is responsible for the maintenance and preservation of creation. Vishnu also goes by many names, which include Ananatasayana, Adita, Padmanabha, Narayana and many others. He has also manifested as incarnations (or avataras) upon earth and also as vyuhas (manifestations), amsavataras (incarnations) and aspects like Panduranga, Varadaraja, Jagannatha, Ranganatha, Venkateswara and many others. India is dotted with many Vishnu temples and those of His numerous incarnations and aspects. Vaikuntha is His abode.

Shiva

Shiva was the most popular deity in the ancient times and was worshipped in diverse communities across the Indian subcontinent (even outside) in many forms. In the last century however, Saivism lost ground to Vaishnavism, but even so, it is still a very popular Hinduism sect with many devoted followers. Just like Vaishnavism, Saivism also has a number of sects and subsects.

The followers of Siva usually worship Him as the supreme Brahman, who's not only responsible for the delusion and liberation of beings, but also the creation, preservation and obliteration of the worlds. Popular Hinduism actually calls him the destroyer.

He has a number of names, which include Rudra, Mahadev, Ishvara, Ardhanariswara and so on. He also has a number of emanations, aspects, manifestations and attendant deities. He is popularly worshipped in households and temples both in his anthromorphic form and Sivalinga form. He is also worshipped in the form of symbols in tantra. His abode is known as Kailās.

Trimurthis

Trimurthis is often translated into English as 'the trinity of the gods of Hinduism'. Shiva, Brahma and Vishnu are often considered to be the Trimurthis. In real life, they embody Brahman's triple functions in creation. They are said to be the same in their highest aspect, but quite different when it comes to their functional aspect, where each rules over a specific sphere and participates in creation together with their attendant deities. Experts often compare them to the Ishvara, Viraj and Hiranyagarbha aspects of Brahman. The reflection of Brahman is Brahma in rajas (activity and passion), Siva in tamas (darkness) and Vishnu in sattva (goodness and purity).

The Premier Goddesses of Hinduism

Shakti

Since the Indus valley civilization, the practice of worshipping the Divine mother was in vogue in India. The word Shakti refers to 'energy.' The Hindus worship Shakti, who is also known as the Mother Goddess, Maya, Prakriti, Divine mother among other names. She embodies the materiality and objectivity in creation; she is thus referred to as Kshetra (the Field). She also embodies the mind and body in the beings. If we talk about Brahman being the instrumental cause of creation, we have to look at Shakti as the material cause. Likewise, if Brahman embodies the consciousness and will, Shakti on the other hand embodies the numerous objects/things, worlds and beings that Brahman's consciousness and will remains hidden in. Shakti is considered the highest reality itself in the Tantra tradition. In this case, Brahman remains as the passive witness consciousness in the background. She is a dependent reality in the Vedic tradition but independent in tantra. Shakti is worshipped in many temples across India as the companion of Shiva.

Saraswathi

Saraswathi (which literally means 'the flowing one') is basically the Hindu goddess of learning and knowledge, and also a consort of Brahma. She embodies our virtue, knowledge and creative intelligence. Being the source of knowledge, she is also the cause of liberation, knowledge and wisdom among all the intelligent beings. She is the one responsible for all artistic expressions, refinement in speech and civilization of behavior. In the ancient past, there was a river that flowed in northwest India which is frequently eulogized as Saraswathi. The civilization that was thriving on the river banks and the adjoining regions is referred to as the Sindhu-saraswadhi civilization. The goddess is responsible for numerous skills and crafts.

There are some depictions that suggest a swan (hamsa) as her vehicle, while others mention peacock. In images, she is typically depicted bearing a vina, which is an Indian musical instrument.

Lakshmi

Lakshmi is the goddess of abundance who's responsible for luck, health, happiness and wealth. She is Lord Vishnu's consort.

Lakshmi was born in the milky oceans during the period when the oceans were churning; she was then gifted to Vishnu. Lakshmi is usually depicted having two or four hands, and either in the company of Vishnu or alone. When alone, she is shown against a background of elephants while standing or seated in a lotus.

As you would expect, she goes by numerous names, but the most popular is Sri. She is said to have incarnated a good number of times upon earth together with Vishnu and participated as the preserver in his duties. Her vehicle is commonly described as an owl. She has multiple forms and the worship of Lakshmi's eight forms (also known as ashta-lakshmis) is a very popular tradition in Hinduism.

Parvathi

Parvathi is the consort of Lord Shiva and goddess of devotion, love and destruction. She is known to personify the many aspects of Mother Goddess and at times is equated with her in her part as the Mother of the Universe. She also features quite prominently in the Kena Upanishad as Uma Haimavathi and is also considered the Mother Goddess' second incarnation after the self-destruction of her first incarnation as Sati or Dakshayani. There are many Shakti pithas set up for the worship of Sati in many parts of India. She goes by a number of names such as Uma, Rudrani, Haimavathi, Durga and Girija.

Parvathi contains both fierce and pleasant aspects and she is described (in some Puranas) as the sister of Vishnu. The images of her usually depict her either alone or together with Shiva.

She is embodied as one half of Siva, the Purusha in the Ardhanarishvara form, as prakriti.

The Vedic Gods and Goddesses

Indra

Indra is acknowledged as the leader of the gods, the chief deity who features in the Vedas prominently and the lord of the heavens. He has a quarter of the Rig-Veda Samhita dedicated to his praise. There are countless hymns that extol him as a mighty warrior that defeated different enemies who include the demon Vrata. He also is said to have cut the wings of mountains with his great weapon, the thunderbolt. In the Upanishads, he is depicted as Brahma's student and

Prataradana, son of Divosa's teacher. Airavat, the white elephant, is considered his vehicle and his consort is Indrani. Nonetheless, this mighty god who was most great in the early Vedic period ended up losing his popularity by the time the Puranas were composed. Ultimately, he ended up being relegated to a fairly inferior place.

Agni

In the Rig-Veda, Agni features very prominently. He has the majority number of hymns addressed to him and he is described as the progeny of the worshippers, the priest, the master of wealth, the messenger, dispeller of the night, provider of wealth, minister of sacrifice and the highest god. His manifests include lightning in the mid-region, fire upon the earth and the sun in the highest realm. The images depict him as a two-headed old man who also has three legs, seven tongues, red body, seven arms, pot belly and four horns. All the arms appear to be holding different objects, and his consorts, Svadha and Svaha, on either side. His vehicle is the ram. He personifies digestive power in the body.

Vayu

Vayu is the wing god who the Vedas describe not only as the lord of the mid region but also a great absorber. He signifies the breath in the body and rides a chariot that is usually drawn by many horses. He also features very prominently in the hymns regarding the Soma sacrifice. He is described as a drinker of Soma and a friend to Indra's. The images depict him as a blue-colored god who has four hands.

Surya

Surya is the sun god and known to be one of the solar deities or Adityas. The Vedic hymns describe him as the flying bird- the foreseeing one, the giver of light, the jewel in the sky and one with radiant hair who has knowledge of all the living and all who traverse the skies and the mid-region, observing all things that give birth. He rides on a chariot with seven horses. Surya is also celebrated as the healer who cures all heart-related diseases and gets rid of the 'yellow hue.'

Varuna

The Vedas describe Varna as the god of clouds, rains, water, oceans and rivers. Many hymns beseech him for forgiveness and protection since he is known to be the guardian of the moral laws and king who observes his people closely, including their actions with countless eyes. He is considered to know all the ways of men and also those of the gods.

There are a good number of hymns that elevate him as the sustainer of the Asvattha tree that has its roots in heaven and branches below, the creator of the wide pathway for the sun to traverse the sky and the highest God.

There are hymns that associate him with Indra (as Indra-Varuna) who is the guardian of men while other hymns associate him with Mitra as Varuna-Mitra.

Existing images depict him as riding either a crocodile or 7 swans containing four hands each holding a conch, a vessel of precious stones, noose and a lotus.

Soma

Also known as Soma Pavamana, Soma is a very important Vedic deity that is highly exalted in some hymns. He has the whole of the ninth mandala of the Rig-Veda dedicated to him. He is also associated with famous Soma Juice, which was ritually extracted from an unknown plant during the soma sacrifices by the Vedic priests. Evidently, it was an intoxicating drink that was used in the rituals to enter into communion or unity with the ancestors as well as the gods. The hymns describe him as the lord of heroes, wise, lord of speech, king, lord of plants the one who leads the ancestors on a straight path and one who creates mortal wise sages. He is believed to have taken part in defeating vrata.

Asvins

Asvins are the twin gods who are well known for their healing ability, and who are always invoked during the sacrificial ceremonies because they are known to always strive to do good to other people. The hymns describe them as surgeons and divine physicians who are well skilled in the art of surgery, healing and even organ transplantation. They are lords of splendor, rich in treasure, having nimble hands, wonder workers, heroes and full of pleasantness, who give blessings or boons to those who worship and seek protection from them.

Aditi

Aditi is known as the prima mother of gods, and particularly the Adityas who are regarded as the 12 solar deities. Aditi is regarded as the prototype of Prakriti or the Mother Goddess, who is usually compared to the sky and space in the Vedas. The hymns have suggested time and again that "she was born to Daksha, who was in turn born to her." There have not been discovered any particular hymns in the Vedas that are directly addressed to her, but she has been mentioned in several hymns together with other gods, such as "the mighty Aditi having the knack to grant Rudra's grace." There is one hymn that describes Aditi as the mother, the heaven, the mid region, all gods, the sons, the five different divisions of men, as well as everything that was actually born and is about to be born. In the Puranas, she is described as the mother of the Indra, Aditya and vanama, and also the wife of sage Kashyapa.

Adityas

The adityas are the solar deities and Aditi's sons who feature in the hymns directly addressed to Rhbus, Visvadevas, agni and many others, and are mentioned together with Rudras, maruts, vasus among other gods of commonality. The Rig-Veda describes them as pure gods, free from blemish, lords of liberal gifts, who assist the worshippers to prosperity, in defeating their enemies and showing the way. Surya is an Aditya, even though he doesn't feature in the list of the Adityas.

Experts speculate that the Adityas were probably the aspects of the same sun or the various suns appearing in the sky during the various hours of the day, and identified with different deities and given different names. Many Rig-Veda hymns mention them together as Aditya without giving their specific names. A number of hymns even distinguish them from Indra, Mitra, Vayu, Brihaspati, Pusan, Bhaga, Surya and Vishnu. Their numbers increased from 8 to 12 in the Puranas, probably due to the split of time into 12 hours instead of 7 or 8. The following 12 Adityas are listed in the Vishnu Puranas: Vivsvat, Amsa, Vishnu, Aryaman, Varuna, Bhaga, Tvstr, Dhuti, Sakra, Savitr Mitra and Pusan.

Usha

The Rig-Veda describes Usha as the goddess of dawn, the radiant daughter of the heavens, daughter of the sky, the auspicious goddess, lady of the light with resplendent rays, opulent goddess, who dawns upon her people with prosperity and who with brilliant light abundantly answers to the prayers.

When you look at the descriptions carefully, you might realize that she may be a precursor to Lakshmi who, like her, rises from the ocean. According to the Rig-Veda, she is the brightest and fairest, Savitr's sister who wakes people up with the sounds of joy and sends great riches to them, and who brings forth all the gods from heaven to drink the Soma.

Yama

Yama is a name that refers to the 'restraining one.' According to the legends, Yama was the first one to die and go to heaven. He subsequently became the lord of the underworld known as Yamaloka. He is believed to have two fierce dogs that have wide nostrils and four eyes that assist him in his duties, which include guarding the path that lead the dead to his world.

In the Puranas, he is described as the ruler of the southern quarter and the god of death, who is known for his fairness, judgement, and knowledge in punishing sinners. The Puranas also describe the various kinds of punishments that are meted out to the sinners in his world, based on the list of sins well recorded by his assistant known as Chitragupta, who's also called the record keeper.

Pusan

Pusan is described in the Chandogya Upanishad as the god of the Sudras. The Rig-Veda portrays him as a solar deity and a guardian of the world who shines in the sky brightly, showing the way to the people on earth and also to the departing souls on their way to the other world. He's referred to as the wonder worker having goats for his steeds and one who drives the path wolves, robbers and other wicked beings away, the lord of prosperity, the one who wields the golden sword and leads people to meadows that are rich in grass. Pusan is also linked with livestock as the one who invigorates them – the one who leads them to green pastures and offers protection to them by assisting men locate their lost cattle. He is described as one of the Adityas in the Puranas.

The other gods include the following:

- Visvadevas
- Rudras
- Maruts
- Brihaspati
- Vasus

Hindus also worship other gods known as Grahas, and also rules and regulations known as Dikpalas. They include the following:

- Navagrahas
- Ashta Dikpalas

The Lesser Divinities

The Hindu religion is diverse. Apart from the major and minor deities, the Hindus also worship a number of local deities, rivers, serpents, village deities, mountains, ancestors, animals and spirits.

Worship of the serpents

The worship of serpents is a common practice in India and images of serpents are usually found in most temples. The women worship live serpents living in their natural habitats located in sacred places or beneath sacred trees, or worship images and status of serpents in the temples. They do so in quest to get boons, for their children, or for the purposes of warding off evil.

Tree worship

There are trees the Hindus consider worthy of worship such as the Banyan tree, Bulrush tree and Pipal tree. The older the tree is, the bigger the faith. Where the tree is located is important because trees that have grown on the banks of sacred streams and rivers or in temples close to the images of major deities usually attract more attention.

River worship

Hindus also worship numerous rivers. There are rivers such as Ganga, Saraswathi, Kshipra, Narmada, Godavari, Yamuna, Kavery, Krishna and Brahmaputra that the Hindus consider sacred and worship on auspicious occasions. Some Hindu customs also call for believers to take a dip in the rivers and use the waters to make offerings to ancestors and gods by either standing in the river or on the banks of these rivers.

Mountain worship

One of the most ancient practices in Hinduism is the worship of mountains and hills and there are many Hindu temples located on the peaks of hills and mountain ranges. The most famous among them include the Arunacala Hill, Mount Kailash,

Tirumala hills, Chamundi Hill and many others. Believers worship them either by offering prayers to their presiding gods or goddesses, making a circumambulation (or Parikrama) around them, or by just visiting the temples on which they are located.

Worship of ancestors

Today, the worship of ancestors is only practiced on a limited scale, in particular communities that are located in areas of Bali, Tamilnadu and Kerala in Indonesia. Nonetheless, the Hindus make offerings ritually according to the traditions to their ancestors on memorial days to ensure their wellbeing and continuity in the world of the ancestors. In the past, it was customary for the Rajput princely families in western and central India to construct temples for their ancestors and worship them. You can still find some of these temples in Jaipur and Indore, among other places.

Worship of seers and saints

A jivanmukta (or a liberated person) in Hinduism is equal to divinity or a god. It is also believed that an enlightened person is god- only in human form and is thus worthy of worship. Since the ancient times, the Hindus have been worshipping seers and saints who spent their lives serving God, or achieved liberation. Examples of the most prominent include Nayanars nad Alvars, a number of teachers including Vyasa, Valmiki, Agastya, Sri Raghavendra of Mantralayam, Mirabai, Basavanna, Gorakshanatha, Ramanujacharya, Sankaracharya and Patanjali. There are also gurus such as Ramakrishna Paramahansa, Bhagavan Nityananda of the Siddha Yoga Tradition, Ramana Maharshi, Paramahansa Yogananda, Shirdi Saibaba and Swami Sivananda Saraswathi. While these gurus may not be worshipped by everyone, their close followers and people who truly believe in them and worship them in great faith.

The worship of sacred objects and symbols

A number of Hindu gods are not just worshipped in their anthropomorphic form, but as symbols and objects too. In Hinduism, there is a lot pf importance placed in the worship of an image as a symbol of the living god. There are very important symbols and objects that the Hindus worship on special occasions or as part of their ritual offerings, which include Poorna Kalasa that symbolizes auspiciousness, fertility, and Divine Mother, Salagrama that symbolizes Vishnu, Shivalinga that symbolizes Parvathi and Shiva embracing closely, footprint images attributed to saintly people or deities, vehicles of gods and goddesses, ornaments that adorn deities in temples, chariots used in temple rituals, elephants that are associated with temples, yantras (or sacred diagrams) usually drawn on the walls or ground of the temples, conches and objects temporarily made of sandal paste, clay or rice balls and domestic animals.

Therefore, you have seen that the Hindus worship everything, literally, from earth to the heavens, the five elements, the human body, sacred self – practically the entire universe. They venerate the whole creation as one and many. Hindus also acknowledge its diversity, duality as well as its unity. The many divinities that are worshipped in Hinduism, as you may have noted, are the manifestations of a single and supreme self.

This God also exists in many forms of Prakriti. All deities worshipped in Hinduism are aspects of Brahman and embody Brahman alone in his ultimate aspect. The fundamental beliefs of Hinduism are justified by the same approach of Hinduism that you can reach God through any path and any deity you choose, so long as your goal is to reach Brahman only, or the greatest and highest supreme, indestructible and indivisible reality.

With that bit of knowledge, I think you are ready to get into the next chapter that talks about the main tenets of Hinduism, and perhaps answers more questions you may be having about the culture and religion of the Hindus.

The Main Tenets of Hinduism

Hinduism is different from many other famous religions with regards to systems and practices. The other famous religions usually have systems and practices that are well defined but Hinduism doesn't really have such a prescribed system of mandated ideas and beliefs. Hinduism is indeed a religion, but also a broad way of life for much of Nepal and India, having an extensive spectrum of practices and beliefs, some of which are similar to primitive pantheism and others embody very deep metaphysical ideals.

As opposed to other religions that contain a specified path to salvation, Hinduism allows and actually encourages many paths to the experience of the divine, and is well tolerant of other religions, looking at them just as different paths to the same goal.

This is an acceptance of variety that makes it very hard to pin down religious tenets that are specific to Hindu; there are however some basic principles that identify Hindu practice and belief that include the following:

The Four Puruṣārthas

The Puruṣārthas refers to the four goals of the life of a human being. Hindus believe that human life needs to seek all four aims, even though persons may have special talents in any one of these Puruṣārthas. They include the following:

Artha

Aratha refers to the quest for material prosperity through practical or constructive work. For the Hindus, this concept includes both traditional work to get daily sustenance as well as government and service to the people.

Dharma

Dharma refers to the ethical, duty-driven way of living in good cooperation with your fellow human beings. This is the path that incorporates a comprehensive set of rules for the proper way of living.

Kama

Kama is the pursuit of happiness and pleasure by exercising passion and desire. Kama doesn't have the suggestion or direct connotation of hedonistic pleasure (as it does in a number of other traditions) but is regarded as a single facet of a spiritual life that is well-rounded.

Moksha

Moksha refers to the quest for salvation and spiritual liberation. This is considered the arena of meditation, together with other forms of mysticism, and scholarly study.

Karma and rebirth

Just like Buddhism, which came from the Hindu philosophy, the Hindu tradition states that the situation you are in today and the outcome in the future is a result or effect of action and consequence.

This belief is held by all the six major Hinduism schools at contrasting levels of literal adherence. Nonetheless, the belief that a person's present situation is always brought about by previous decisions and actions unites these schools. They also believe that the circumstances in the future are the natural outcome of the decisions and actions made at the moment. Whether rebirth or karma from one lifetime to the next one are seen as literal, the deterministic events, or mental depictions of living by consequences, Hinduism as a religion does not lean on the notion of divine grace, but on the merits of actions made at free will. According to the Hindu teachings, you are who you are based on what you've done; thus, what you do today determines what you'll be.

Samsara and Moksha

In Hinduism, it is believed that rebirth is the condition of samsara, and that the life's ultimate goal is moksha, or nirvana, which is the realization of your own relationship with God, the attainment of the inner peace and detachment from all concerns of this world. With this realization, you get freed from samsara and the rebirth and suffering cycle is ended. While there are schools of Hinduism that think that moksha is a psychological condition that can be achieved on earth, other schools think that moksha is another worldly liberation occurring after death.

The Soul

Hinduism has quite a complicated belief system with respect to the individual soul, and also to the universal soul that can be thought of as one deity - God.

According to Hinduism, all creatures have a soul, or a true self referred to as atman. This soul is different and distinct from the supreme and universal soul known as Brahman. The goal in life is to discover and recognize that your soul is identical to the supreme soul and also that the supreme soul exists everywhere and that all life is linked to oneness.

The Four Stages of Life

In Hinduism, there is a belief that human life is divided into four stages (or four plus three); these are just like the goals of life, with the three deriving from a strand of Hinduism holding that "life is good" and the other one deriving from the strand holding that "life is bad" and each stage has defined rituals and rites from birth to death.

- The first stage is referred to as the student stage, or Brahmacharya.
- The second stage is the Householder stage, or Grihastha.
- The third is the hermit stage, or Vanaprastha.
- The fourth stage is the Wandering Ascetic stage, or Sannyasa.

Progressing Through Life in the Three Stages

The three life stages that come from the life-affirming Vedic state of Hinduism were designed initially with the caste system in mind. Particularly, they were created to apply to members of the three varnas (or the Hindu castes) that include the Kshatriya, the Brahmin and Vaishya - these are known as the "twice born" varnas, or the upper three castes whose males (who've come of age -at 12 years) undergo a 're-birth' ceremony.

The other jatis (sub-castes) and castes have adopted them in various ways, changing them to meet their needs.

The First Stage- The Student

In the first stage, the boy is traditionally expected to go live and study with a teacher or guru for a number of years. Unfortunately, this tradition is followed fully only in a few Brahmin families. When a boy reaches adolescence (at about 8-12 years of age), he gets into student-hood and spends most of his maturing years studying. If the boy is Brahmin, for instance, it means learning and memorizing the Vedas along with the accompanying text, together with training in the various rituals. Adherents of all castes learn about setting up and maintaining their household worship that's centered on the holy fire of Agni.

For the castes who are "born-twice," the samskara, or ritual of becoming a student, has a lot of importance since it is the means by which the individual becomes reborn. This ceremony is often referred to as the thread ceremony because the initiate wears a red thread over his left shoulder, symbolizing the entrance of the boy into Hinduism; originally, this was the point at which the initiate was first allowed to hear the words of the sacred Vedas and learn his first mantra. After being initiated, the boy joined the other "twice-born" males who are responsible for keeping the balance of the cosmos.

After the student hood, the individual enters the next stage of life known as the householder.

Second Stage- The Householder

This stage is usually entered into through an elaborate marriage ceremony that takes quite a number of days. In this stage, a man has children with his wife and creates a family. He also establishes himself in a career or job and endeavors to be an active community member. The man establishes his household that has its own worship. Together with his wife, the householder is now responsible for ensuring that various rituals that entail domestic life are performed properly. This very important stage is responsible for supporting as well as looking after other people (both male and female) in all the other stages.

The Third Stage- Retirement

The third stage of life is when the man grows old, when he has an adult son who already has a family and is interested and ready to take up the leadership role in the household. It means that the man and his wife have to retire. During this stage, their religious and secular household responsibilities diminish significantly. What's more, both become free to think about the meaning of their imminent death and rebirth. They have the option of withdrawing into a secluded place - maybe decide to become a 'hermit' - or take part in more active worship of the pantheon of gods and goddesses in Hinduism.

Each one of these three stages is led by a samskara, or a ritual that brings an individual from the previous stages of life into the new one. These are indeed the most important stages of life, brought on by very elaborate samskaras, but there are many other samskaras conducted during the life of an individual. According to the traditions, an individual may undergo anywhere from 10 to 18 or even about 40 samskaras in their entire lifetime, and the majority of them are conducted before a baby reaches six months old, with a good number of them conducted before birth. In Hinduism, they are believed to assist a person to leave behind their previous life and enter into a new one successfully. Each samskara further advances a person along the path of life, while initiating them into any fresh aspect/stage.

Clearly, life's three stages are created for males and have no place for women. Just like many other religions, traditional Hinduism places women in a dependent role. When we look at the traditional view, women always require the protection of a responsible male, whether husband, father or adult son, but you should note that this does not mean that a woman has no religious life. Quite the contrary, women are expected to be involved in worship very actively - both to support their family and for their own gain. What's more, a married woman is responsible for performing many of the domestic rites together with her husband. There are many rituals that cannot be conducted without her taking part, or, in some cases, leadership. Women are usually active practitioners of some forms of the worship of gods and goddesses or bakhti yoga.

In the modern era though, this subordination has begun changing and women have gotten more active roles in public life. Take Indira Ghandi for instance; for many years, she was a Prime Minister of India.

The Fourth Stage- Rejecting Life

This stage of life essentially breaks the progression of the other three and is that of the ascetic who the Hindus call sannyasin or sadhu. This stage entails a rejection of life and all its meaning in trade for a quest to attain moksha, which is the process of being released from a cycle of samsara. You may enter into this life stage at any time.

The rejection of life, and particularly as the life-affirming strand of Hinduism defines it, is complete. It needs an individual to reject all the household responsibilities and duties of all the stages of life. What's more, the individual has to reject all the religious beliefs. There is a ceremony of making one a sannayasin, which consists of burning of the Vedas copies as a symbolic rejection even of the individual's role in maintaining the cosmos, and also of one's red thread or the symbol of their status as "twice-born." This rejection is so powerful that a person can even lose his caste affiliation; indeed, even a shudra can become a sannyasin and drop his low-caste identity.

The sannyasins live life without any possessions or shelter – they become wandering hermits. They only eat when they can get food but never work to eat it; this means that the individual has to find it or receive it from someone. On the other hand, they become holy men and seek spiritual enlightenment and power, endeavoring to attain the true wisdom of the cosmos. There are some who may choose to be kind and bless those around them, but there are others who may become powerful and wrathful and use magic against people who cross them.

Let's discuss some aspects of the chapter above in more detail in the following exciting chapter as we learn more about the Hindu culture.

The Hindu Rites of Passage

Birth

Before the birth of a baby, Hindus recite prayers and perform rituals to protect the fetus from harmful spirits and illness. The mother then ensures she eats healthy foods only to ensure the newborn is healthy and safe. In some families, the baby's father conducts a ceremony right after the birth by dipping a golden pen into a jar of honey and writes "Om" - the secret Sanskrit symbol - onto the tongue of the infant. The symbol stands for truth and is written with hopes that the child will grow to be honest and speak the truth which is known to be as sweet as honey.

After a while (a week or so), the baby is given a name formally. Typically, the name of a desired or favorite goddess or god is selected and whispered into the ear of the child. If the child is a girl, she undergoes an ear-piercing ceremony within the first few years of her life. The hair is also cut (for both boys and girls), symbolic of the renewal and the shedding of transgressions in lives of the past.

The sacred thread ceremony

This ceremony is a rite of passage that dates as far back as the ancient times. It marks passage into adolescence and is reserved for the male members of the Brahmins, Vaishyas and Shatriyas (the three upper castes). It embodies a birth or initiation into the religious community, much like the Jewish bar mitzvah.

This rite of passage is traditionally served to introduce into religious life the devotee. The young man shaves his head in the presence of a holy teacher or guru and wears a saffron robe. Then he takes just a simple walking stick after which he proceeds to renounce all his material possessions then receives a special 'sacred thread.' This thread (which is usually adorned) is meant to symbolize how different things are closely interconnected. It is made up of seven strands and each of them represents a different quality or virtue. They include the following:

- Intelligence
- Memory
- Power of speech
- Forgiveness
- Steadfastness
- Good reputation
- Prosperity

The boy then promises to represent these qualities and wears the sacred thread for the rest of his life as a symbol that he has come to age.

To conclude the ceremony, there is a fire sacrifice which is the most common form of Hindu ritual. In the past, the person being initiated had to follow their teacher into a faraway place to study the Holy Scriptures and live a life made up of spiritual practice and austerity. After that, he would go back to the society, get married and raise a family. Today, it is only the young men looking to become priests or ascetics who live with gurus.

Marriage

Most marriages in Hinduism are organized by the parents, although the children have to first be happy with their chosen partners. The Hindus typically marry someone who is in the same caste although the modern period has seen a growing number of exceptions. In Hinduism, a wedding is important, and is one of the most colorful ceremonies. While customs may vary in the different regions, among Hindus marriages are always full of joy and regarded as momentous occasions full of decorations and food. As a matter of fact, some Hindu weddings tend to go as long as three days.

The marriage ceremony is done around a sacred fire that is considered god Agni's manifestation. The couple's friends and family surround them, then a priest chants some Sanskrit verses before leading the bride and groom around the flames burning in a brick fire pit. What follows is the sounding of the bells and numerous offerings are made to the fire, including flowers, clarified butter and grains. Each time the couple finishes their circuit, the bride goes ahead to stand on one of the bricks, to affirm her strength and loyalty.

Lastly, the groom and his bride go around the flames in seven steps. These steps are the most important part of a Hindu wedding. At this point, the couple is bonded for life and their union is officially sanctified.

Death

Cremation (the burning of dead bodies) has always been a Hindu custom since the ancient times. The rite of passage into the world of the dead incorporates the sacred fire, much like the marriage ceremony. The funeral starts when the corpse is wrapped in a piece of cloth, placed on a stretcher and carried away. As the friends and family start leaving their village for the cremation area, they begin reciting prayers to the selected deity of the deceased. According to the traditions, the eldest son has to light the wood of the funeral fire using a flame lit in a temple nearby. With the people believing that the deceased is going through a rebirth process (since the fire cleanses him/her into a new life), offerings and prayers are made. The ritual is also done to protect the relatives from evil spirits.

To close the ritual, ashes are thrown into a river. Many Hindus have always preferred their remains to be placed in the River Ganges - they believe that its waters will assist in purifying their souls.

Other rituals

The Hindu world of rituals offers some common features that tie all Hindus into a bigger Indian religious system and influence other religions too, even though the manifestations of the rituals differ to a large extent among individuals, villages and regions.

Before we continue, there's something important I feel I ought to mention here.

According to me, the division between pollution and purity is the most outstanding feature in religious ritual. Religious acts assume a level of impurity (or defilement) for the practitioner, which need to be neutralized or overcome either before or during the ritual procedures.

Purification, which is usually done with water, is therefore a typical feature in most religious practices. Another feature of the Hindu ritual is the avoidance of impure things. This includes taking the life of an animal, associating with dead things, or even body fluids, and eating flesh. Purification is thus important for repressing pollution.

In the Hindu society, the people who are able to avoid the impure are usually given a lot of respect.

Another significant feature is the belief in the efficacy of sacrifice, which includes survivals of the Vedic sacrifice. Therefore, sacrifices can incorporate the conducting of offerings in a well-regulated way, along with the preparation of sacred space, manipulation of objects and recitation of texts.

Third, there is another feature known as the concept of merit that is gained through the conduct of good works such as charity that mounts up over time and eventually reduces the sufferings in the next world.

The other common rituals include the following:

1. Domestic worship

Most Hindus usually engage in worship and various religious rituals in the homes. The down is highly regarded as the most important time of the day for people to do various household rituals, even though devout families may engage in devotion more frequently.

For most Hindu households, the day starts when the women start drawing auspicious geometric designs anywhere on the floor or on the doorstep using rice flour or rice.

The orthodox Hindus, however, start with a recitation of the Rig-Veda (during dawn and dusk) of the Gayatri Mantra for the sun, which is the only Sanskrit prayer many people know.

What follows is a bath, and then a personal worship of the gods at the family shrine. This usually includes lighting a lamp and offering pieces of food before the images while reciting prayers in the regional language or Sanskrit.

During the evenings, particularly in the rural areas, the female devotees come together for lengthy sessions of praise to the gods or goddesses and singing hymns.

To punctuate the day, they Hindus hold minor acts of charity, and other bouts of rituals such as offering some water in memory of the ancestors during the daily baths. During each meal, families may set aside some grain to donate to the needy people, and daily gifts of little amounts of grains to the birds and other animals; this is seen as an act of self-sacrifice that is meant to mount up merit for the family.

2. The unusual rituals

Just like any other religions in the world, Hinduism does have some weird rituals and practices which are also considered integral to the Hindu society and religion. Let's take a peek at some of them.

Fire-walking

There is a festival in South India, known as the Theemithi festival, in which people from South India celebrate by walking across a pit packed with burning firewood barefoot. Glowing charcoal is at times used. This is a ritual done to honor Draupati Amman, a Hindu goddess. The devotees are harshly discouraged from hurrying across the pit as they are supposed to do it slowly as though they are walking in the park.

To start the ritual off, the head priest fills a pot with 'sacred' water and places it on his head and traverses the pit. Other men (seeking to prove their devotion by enduring the pain) follow him. The participants definitely suffer from burns on their feet which sometimes turn into really bad injuries which are worsened when they fall into the red-hot pit.

Hooking

Another really weird festival is the famous Thookam festival in which the devotees accept their backs to be pierced by sharp hooks. When the hooks are firmly placed on their backs, they are lifted using ropes off the ground onto a scaffold. To increase the pressure and pain, children are at times tied to the participants' hands and suspended. This practice originates from the southern region of India. Currently, though, the festival has been banned by the Government of India after the mounting pressure from the Human Rights organizations against the practice.

Bull fighting

Also known as Jallikattu, the Indian bull-fighting is a popular practice in Hinduism. Bull fighting is actually done without the aid of any weapons or ropes (thus being very different from its Spanish counterpart). Luckily, the life of the bull is spared after the practice - bovines are extremely sacred in India. It goes without saying that this is the most dangerous sporting activity done in India, and it is celebrated during the harvest thanksgiving or Pongal.

The youth, desperately ardent for some glory, typically strive to either tame the bull or hang on to it at least to get a little reward, which is usually in form of money.

Famous as it may be, bull fighting has led to the death of more than a hundred people in southern India over the last two decades, perhaps the reason for the current considerations of banning the sport. Well, in case you're wondering, the bulls are fed on alcohol forcefully, their eyes sprinkled with hot pepper and testicles pinched to make them as infuriated as possible before the ritual.

Widow burning

This ritual known as Sati was extensively practiced in the 17th century. The ritual entailed the voluntary or involuntary participation of a widow – she was required to lie next to her dead husband, then, together with the corpse, she would be set ablaze. Of course, there were widows who would be caught trying to escape 'their fate' despite the excessive social pressure to immolate themselves; in such cases, the limbs of these widows would be dislocated and broken, or simply tied to the burning structure to prevent more attempts to escape. In some instances, they would be pushed back into the burning funeral pyre with bamboo sticks.

The British colonial Government banned the practice in 1859 but some parts of India still continued practicing it. Today it is still banned by the Indian Government and harsh penalties are imposed on the people who insist on continuing with this practice.

Note:

According to Hindu belief systems, the Sati or "faithful wife" (based on the original meaning of the Sanskrit word) died as a wife and eschewed the ill-fated, ill-omened state of widowhood: along with the "belief effect" of the ritual, the "eye of faith" makes the joint cremation of wife and husband appear to the onlookers (as well as to the sati) to be a holy renewal of their marriage ceremony. Through the sacrifice, the sati is able to preserve the spiritual and bodily unity of the couple and ultimately, give the Hindu sacrament its definitive and realest expression.

Food rolling

When you enter particular temples in Karnataka, you'll be given an order to halt, drop and begin rolling. The different supplicants usually roll their bodies down over the scraps of foods that Brahmins have discarded. Brahmins is the greatest priestly case in India. This ritual, which is said to cure disease, is practiced by all the castes that are lower than Brahmin.

This practice is known as 'made snana' and it has been around for over five centuries. Following the increasing calls to ban or restrict this practice, there were restrictions put up in particular temples but were shortly lifted when various devotees protested. The members of the Indian government have instead opted to use a different approach to help people find reason to change their ways instead of imposing their will on people.

Exorcism

In Hinduism, there have been different ways of conducting exorcism rituals, and one of them is the famous slaughtering of a white chicken. When a white chicken is slaughtered, its bloody parts are strewn strategically by the Priest or Pandit placed in charge of conducting the exorcism. The possessed individual is then either addressed by the name of a departed relative (who may have become an evil demon within the individual) or as a demon.

According to the traditional beliefs, the spirits or demons are usually afraid of white chickens, and in some instances the demon is reported to have cried, "I go, I go!" through the body of the possessed person before leaving. This is supposedly followed by the instant revival of the exorcised individual who appears to wake up from some form of trance without any memory of the events or the white chicken.

In the Hindu tradition, the practices and beliefs relating to the practice of exorcism are conspicuously connected with the ancient Dravidians living in the south. The Atharva Veda, which is part of the four Vedas, is held to contain secrets pertaining to medicine and magic and many spells described in the book are specifically designed to cast out evil spirits and demons. These beliefs are very strong and are currently practiced in Orissa, West Bengal and the southern states such as Kerala. The basic techniques of exorcism that are used in the Tantric ad Vedic traditions are yajnaf and mantra.

In the Vaishnava traditions, there is also a recitation of names of the Narasimha (one of the avatars of Vishnu, who appeared to save the world from a demon figure in the ancient times) and reading scriptures such as Bhagavata Purana loudly. Garuda Purana is the main Vedic resource on ghost information and other death related information.

Even today, mantras are being used in the exorcism of evil spirits and protection from their harm. For instance, with regards to sleep paralysis (a condition in which you are unable to speak or move in bed, yet are still very conscious for a few seconds or minutes), which the ancient Hinduism associates with evil spirits, one of the most regarded solutions lie in "Gau Mata Mantra" which practitioners refer to as the 'invocation of positive energy.' The process of this mantra involves waking up in the morning and bowing to the feet of a Desi cow with a hump (Gau Mata) and reciting a mantra before offering her some fresh Indian bread (known as roti) or Gau Mata fodder.

Apart from what we've discussed above, I'm sure you've wondered about other aspects of Hinduism. In the next section, we are going to look at some of the most asked questions about the culture, religion or general practices of Hinduism.

The Common Questions Usually Asked About Hinduism
1. Why Do the Hindus Wear A Dot On Their Foreheads?

The Hindus wear the dot on their foreheads mainly as a religious symbol. The dot represents divine sight; it also shows that the person wearing it is a Hindu. For the women, the dot doubles as a beauty mark.

In the Hindi language, the dot is referred to as bindi, or Bindu in Sanskrit. During the ancient times, all the Hindu men and women used to wear these marks along with earrings, but today the women are the ones who are most faithful in wearing the bindi.

Moreover, the dot is believed to contain a mystical meaning. It embodies the spiritual sight's third eye, which is able to see what the physical eyes cannot. Even as the Hindus seek to use yoga to awaken their inner sight, the dot reminds them to use and nurture this spiritual vision to perceive and understand the inner workings of life better - to see things not just 'physically,' but also with the "mind's eye."

What is the dot made of?

The bindi is made of sindur, or red pepper, which is made traditionally from fresh lime juice and powdered turmeric, cosmetics or sandal paste.

Are there other similar marks?

Yes. Apart from the simple dot, the Hindus have other different types of forehead marks, referred to as tilaka in Sankrit. Each mark represents a particular denomination or sect of the vast Hindu religion which we mentioned in the previous chapters. The Vaishnava, for instance, wear a V-shaped tilaka that's essentially made from white clay. More elaborate tilakas are worn mainly at religious events even though many wear the simple bindi to show that they are Hindu, even in the general public. We therefore know what an individual believes by these marks, which is important in informing us how to start conversations.

NOTE:

The red Bindi is also a sign of marriage. An individual may wear a black bindi before marriage to protect against the "evil eye."

Sometimes it may also be used as an exotic fashion statement where the color of the dot complements with the color of the lady's sari.

2. Why Do the Hindus Worship The Cow?

It is said that millions of Hindus worship the cow. Well, if you thought so, you need to understand that Hinduism is a religion that lifts the status of the Mother to the level of Goddess. The cow is not worshipped but is revered and considered sacred: it provides human beings with life sustaining milk; the cow is a maternal figure and a care taker of the people. The cow is seen as a symbol of the earth's divine bounty.

Among the most popular deities of Hinduism is Lord Krishna. He is usually depicted playing a flute and dancing amongst cows. He is believed to have grown up as a cow herder. Krishna also has other names - Gopala and Govinda, which mean protector and friend of the cows (literally). The Hindus consider it highly auspicious for a devotee to feed the cow before having his or her own breakfast.

The Vedic scriptures have multiple verses emphasizing that the cow must be protected and well taken care of; it is thus considered a sin to slaughter a cow and consume its meat. There are many states in the modern India which have illegalized the slaughter of cow, and for that reason, you will often find cows roaming freely all over India including the busy streets of Mumbai and Delhi.

Ayurveda is a big advocate of the sattvic qualities of dairy products and milk and that's why you'll find most Hindus being vegetarian but not vegan. Apart from their milk, though, the cows are also useful for numerous practical purposes, and are considered very important to the rural populace. The bulls are used to plough the farm fields and transport goods. Lord Shiva's trusted vehicle is actually the sacred bull that's known as Nandi.

In a religious land as India, you will find religious ceremonies taking place at any place. Spiritual 'yagnas,' or fire ceremonies, are some of the most popular ones that are usually performed to thank the gods and ask for their blessings; cows have an integral role to play in these yagnas.

Lastly, the Ayurveda knows that some physical and emotional health crises can't be healed solely by herbs and diet. They require the deeper and more subtle healing of these kinds of Vedic ritual ceremonies to be able to clear 'astrological' ancient karma. Once again, the holy cow provides its bounty by offering the ingredients in the blessed milk, or Panchamrit, that's distributed once the ceremony is over. The word Panchamrit literally translates to 'nectar of the gods' or 'sacred ambrosia.' It is made up of five ingredients which include milk, honey, ghee, yoghurt and sugar. When you drink this sweet concoction, you are infused with the divine energy made during the puja, and healed.

3. Why Do Some Hindu Deities Have Animal Features?

The different Gods in the wide-ranging traditions of Hinduism usually have distinct forms and personalities based on the way they have been seen in visions and how they are depicted in legends and stories. Hindus do not necessarily feel the need to question the fact, for example, that Lord Ganesha is depicted having the head of an elephant. Is it that he chose that form to have himself distinguished as the lord of obstacles? Nobody really knows. The important fact is that masses of Hindus worship and get blessings from the benevolent elephant daily. Many Hindus who are perhaps looking for an explanation know that Ganesha is a real being who looks like an elephant. Other people believe that the elephant is symbolic, and even more are content with the legends or ancient stories in the Puranas that explain how Ganesha came to have an elephant head. Quite interestingly though (and maybe due to his endearing appearance), Ganesha is seen as the most popular Hindu deity in Hinduism. Many other divinities in Hinduism have animal attributes, including Varuna, Kamadhenu, Hanuman, the vahanas (the gods' animal mounts), four of the ten incarnations of Vishnu (boar, fish, turtle, half-man-half-lion) and the Nagas.

4. Why Is It That the Ordinary Spoken Language Cannot Be Used Instead Of Sanskrit During Worship? This Would Assist Us to Understand and Follow The Rites Better!

Worship (or Pita), sacrifice (Homa), and other religious rites like that are usually considered sacred and holy in Hinduism. The sages (rishis) who are the originators of religious traditions brought these rites to the Hindus, which include the right procedures and the mantras to be used. Therefore, it is only appropriate that the Hindus conform strictly to the pattern of the rites and the language of their transmission to them. This produces a sacred and solemn atmosphere.

What's more, we have the science of the mantras which asserts that the different mantras used in the rites contain a special potency. When pronounced and intoned well, they bring forth a salutary effect on the minds of the people hearing them. Thus, if Hindus use translations or versions in the spoken language, they remain merely as translations and don't act at all as mantras.

Nonetheless, I think it would be of use if a general description of the rites and the real meaning of mantras are delivered first in the spoken language, followed by the rituals in a traditional way. The rites would become more comprehensible to the votaries.

You should also not forget here that in other religions too, the religious rites and ceremonies are usually performed in the language of the original scriptures.

5. Are Converts Accepted in Hinduism?

We have had incidents in the past that have shown that Hinduism does not really take in or embrace converts fully. For instance, there was an American woman who wanted to marry an Indian man. She first got converted into Hinduism and everything was fine until some years ago when she was denied entry into the 11th century Lingaraj Temple. This issue created quite a scene outside the temple as her husband insisted she be allowed in. There was a board outside the temple which would not accept any entry for non-Hindus, and even though her husband insisted that his wife was a Hindu, the priests refused to change their minds.

Many Hindus would tell you that according to them, there is nothing wrong even if you were a non-Hindu and wanted to enter a temple, even if it is a 'high' temple. However, every temple is managed by some people who make the rules - it is okay if they do, as long as the rules are in line with the core principles of Hinduism, and that they don't harm the image of Hinduism.

I also wondered if there was any truth or logic behind the apparent fact that Hinduism doesn't allow converts. Is it that the fact that Hindus don't try converting non-Hindus can explain why converts are generally not accepted?

We can find the understanding for the main reason why Hindus don't attempt to convert in three key Hinduism teachings. These are reincarnation, casteism and karma.

Each one of them buttress each other in believing that all men are on a path (at differing distances) from achieving release from samsara into moksha. Thus, in a sense, Hinduism believes that there isn't any need of trying to convert somebody. In other words, individuals not born as Hindus ultimately, through rebirth, become Hindus so long as they live properly. This would be a great idea for any religion as it assumes that a Hindu is at the peak of the heap of reincarnation. If you think about it, if one went by this, everybody would be well on their way to becoming a Hindu, including individuals who are outside the belief system. It's only that they have not yet gotten there. The people who are not there yet are really not Hindus – they are not ready to become Hindus.

One guru stated that, "When you die while you are not a Hindu, it is not a real concern to Hindus for the simple fact that they believe that such people will perhaps be born into another life in a new form. Ultimately, if they live right, they will automatically ascend through the various life forms to humanity and then to a high caste before reaching moksha eventually."

Karma is meant to sort this out.

According to me though, converts are accepted in Hinduism and the claims that converts are not true Hindus is not entirely true.

According to Swami Vivekananda, "*Conversion of an individual from other religions into Hinduism is very normal. It has taken place time and again and should anyway. I'm sure you've heard that Hinduism is not a proselytizing religion, that Hindu really never tries to convert other people, that you have to be born a Hindu to be a Hindu or be born in India to achieve the same. These are ridiculous notions. After doing some bit of research to try and trace the person who came up with this sort of thinking..., after making a note of every comment, we realized that it was entirely Christian propaganda. On the other hand, the writes of statement affirming that Hindus bringing other people into their faith were prominent Hindus.*"

Comparison Between Buddhism and Hinduism

Well, this was supposed to be addressed as one of the questions, however, considering the number of times the question has been asked by people outside the two religions, and the number of people within both that have always sought a good answer, I thought it better to have it as a chapter.

Let's begin by an introduction and meaning of Buddhism first.

A Buddha is a person who has attained wisdom (or Bodhi), an ideal state of ethical and intellectual perfection that only by human means can a person achieve. The word Buddha literally translates to the 'enlightened one' - a knower. According to Buddhists, a Buddha is born in every aeon of time and the Buddha, known as sage Gotama, who achieved enlightenment at Buddh Gaya in India under the bo tree was seventh in the succession.

In efforts to explain Buddhism, a story is always told:

Gotama was a son of a King in India on the border of modern Nepal about 632 years before Christ (of Christianity) was born. The seers foresaw that he would either become a Buddha or an emperor, but since his father wanted him to become an emperor, he made sure he was kept away from all unpleasant things so that he might not see life and become wise. Buddhism holds that the gods knew that this man had to become the Buddha, so they gave earth a visit in different forms to let him witness them. Gotama, on three successive days, saw an old man, an ill man and a dead body (while on his way to a park) and thus learnt that all men must suffer and eventually die. On the fourth day, he saw a monk and he understood from that that in order to learn the way of overcoming the universal sorrows of man, one must give up the worldly pleasures. He thus renounced his kingdom at twenty-nine years old and became an ascetic.

Gotama started wandering about in the countryside to seek truth and peace. He approached many great teachers of his day but none of them could offer him what he pursued. He practiced all the severe austerities of monkish life strenuously and hoped to attain Nirvana. His delicate body was eventually reduced to a skeleton and the more his body got tormented, the more he strayed from his goal. He realized the futility of self-mortification and finally decided to follow a different course, in which he avoided the extremes of indulgence and pain.

This new path he found was the 'middle way,' or the eightfold path, which soon became part of his teaching. His wisdom developed into its fullest power when he followed this path and he became the Buddha.

Prince Gautama, as a man, by his own wisdom, will and love, attained Buddhahood - the most supreme state of human perfection, known as enlightenment. After his enlightenment, he then started teaching his followers to actually believe that they could do the same.

NOTE:

According to experts of History, Hinduism could even date back to more than 5000 years but the origin of Hinduism came into existence in a much later period. After the Lord Buddha attained enlightenment, he preached everything he learnt from all his experiences. Everything he taught is what ended up being known as Buddhism and people received them well. During the latter part of the Vedic period, Hinduism was on the verge of declining due to the superstitions, orthodoxy and staunch practices that prevailed in the region. Buddhism came in with lesser rituals and complexities and was accepted by the people of India. It was during this time that Buddhism came out of the atheistic strands of Hinduism. It is an undeniable fact, however, that Buddhism evolved and grew because of the complex nature that was quickly evolving in Hinduism, but even though they have a number of differences, both have quite a lot of things in common.

Teachings of Dhamma

All the Buddha teachings are usually summarized in one word: Dhamma, which means truth or that which really is. It also refers to law, the law that exists in the heart and mind of a man. We can call it the principle of righteousness. Thus, the Buddha appeals to a man to be pure, noble and charitable, not so that he can please any supreme deity, but so that he can be true to the highest in himself. Dhamma, the law of righteousness, also exists in the universe and the whole universe is an epitome and revelation of Dhamma. *"By the rising and setting of the moon, the coming of rain, the changing of seasons we know that Dhamma exists – Dharma is a law of the universe that actually makes matter act in the ways which the studies of natural science reveal."* It is believed that if a man lives by Dhamma, he escapes misery and comes to Nirvana - the ultimate release from all forms of suffering. A man will discover Dhamma not by prayer or ceremonies, or appeal to a god but through developing his own character which can only be achieved by controlling the mind and purification of emotions.

"Buddhism is not a religion"

This therefore means that Buddhism is not at all a religion - in the sense in which we commonly understand the word. There is no such thing as a belief in a 'body of dogma' which believers must be taken on faith. For instance, the belief in a supreme being, the creator of the cosmos or even the reality of a soul that never dies. Buddhism starts as a search for truth. According to the teachings of the Buddha, we should only believe something that is true, judging by our own experience, that which is in conformity to reason and is favorable to the highest good and well-being of all beings.

So far, I think you can point out some differences and similarities now that you understand a bit of what Buddhism is all about. Let's continue.

Rebirth, samsara and reincarnation

As you may have noted, both Hinduism and Buddhism believe in an endless cycle of different births that are known as samsara, and both search for release from seemingly endless cycles of rebirths.

According to the Hindus, we have an eternal soul (or atman) that's reincarnated intact from birth to birth. If you can remember, we mentioned earlier that the Hindus seek release (liberation or moksha) through spiritual practice so that the soul can unite with the universal divine force or Brahman.

Buddha taught that that living beings are made up of a collection of feelings, senses, perceptions and other intangibles and not a constant soul. This concept of the lack of a constant, existing soul is referred to as anatta. Thus, the ultimate goal for Buddhists is largely abstract - escaping the cycle of rebirths to end suffering, and entering into a state of Nirvana (a cool place in which a person is far from the fires of kleshas or defilement and desire).

NOTE:

Kleshas are states of the mind that are known to cloud the mind and manifest in actions that are unpleasant, such as anger, anxiety, depression, jealousy and fear.

Cause and effect

Both Hinduism and Buddhism believe in Karma, which states that the actions of our past affect our present and states of our future life. This means that according to both sides, you could do evil in the current life and be born again as a cockroach in the next life. Likewise, the afflictions you face in this life are usually explained away as the consequences of Karma from your previous life or transgressions earlier in this life.

The way of life or Dharma

Dharma is a word common to both Hinduism and Buddhism. The Buddhists typically use the word to refer to the collection of teachings of the Buddha, and the Buddha coarsely used the word Dharma to mean 'how the universe operates.' According to Hinduism, the concept of Dharma is usually thought to mean 'the role of a person in the universe.' The concept includes not only the performance of religious acts of a person, but how they behave in the society, and how they act toward the responsibilities of their families.

An individual's dharma, in a Hindu society, may differ based on their caste as well as the different stages of life that they are in. For instance, a boy from a lower caste might have a completely different dharma compared to an old man from a higher caste.

Devotion to God

As you already know, Hinduism has thousands of goddesses and gods, but we can look at the religion as monotheistic, for the most part, since we saw that each god is a manifestation of the one supreme God. We also saw that each Hindu family is devoted to a particular deity and most Hindus practice bhakti (devotion) to either a form of Lord Shiva or Lord Vishnu, seeing this as a very important part of religious practice.

The Buddha, on the other hand, taught that Buddhists ought not to concern themselves with worship or devotion to any particular God. You should note that the Buddha didn't explicitly deny that a supreme God existed, but asserted that we are solely responsible for our personal enlightenment. We should not believe that some supreme being will help us.

The Buddha didn't decry or criticize the devotional acts to the gods and goddesses and animal sacrifices that were normal. In the end, this belief or faith in the sacredness of life spread to Hinduism, and instead of becoming the norm, animal sacrifice became the exception. Actually, the impact of Buddha on Hinduism was so strong that most followers of Vishnu believe that Buddha was one of the ten avatars of Vishnu, even though Buddhists do not share the belief.

Meditation and yoga

Both Hinduism and Buddhism strongly believe in growing awareness and mental concentration in the spiritual quest. In Buddhism, meditation is close to ubiquitous, with insight meditation, or Vipassana, being the most underscored form of meditation. The monks of Buddhism are expected to spend hours every day meditating; the lay people are only expected to practice regularly, and can go to meditation sessions at the local temples. The Metta, or compassion meditation, is also emphasized by the Mahayana Schools of Buddhism.

Hinduism, on the other hand, regards yoga as more than a series of postures to be held as a form of exercise. Instead, yoga (or yoke – or "to be yoked by God") is made up of different practices as highlighted below:

- Observing of tolerance and self
- Abstention form transgressions like greed, theft, dishonesty and violence
- The postures or Asana that are practiced globally
- Meditation
- Breath control

- Mental concentration and calming (stilling) the mind
- Withdrawal of senses

Tantric practices

Buddhism has a large sect, known as "Tantrayana," which is largely based upon the practices of tantra.

In Hinduism, tantric practices are quite prevalent, particularly among the devotees of the god Shiva and goddess Kali.

The Mahayana Buddhism believes that the Buddha's original teachings are from the practices of Hinduism, which include prayers and the concept of God. Mahayana Buddhism introduces the idea of heavens and hells too.

Asceticism

In Hinduism, it is accepted that extreme asceticism is the way, but in Buddhism (like we said earlier), the middle way is ideal - Buddhism rejects any form of extreme asceticism and great wealth.

The vedas

The Buddhists don't generally believe in the Vedas. On the contrary, they believe in the teachings of Lord Buddha and Buddhist scriptures.

When it comes to Hinduism, the supremacy of the four Vedas: Samveda, Rigveda, Atharvaveda and Yajurveda are upheld.

The stages of life

In Buddhism, there is no belief in any stages of life. Buddhists can join any stage they wish any time, but it is based on their spiritual preparedness.

Hinduism, on the other hand, does believe in the four 'ashramas,' or stages of life (Brahmacharaya Ashram, Grihastha Ashram, Vanprastha Ashram and Sanyasa Ashram).

Conclusion

There's a lot more to learn about Hinduism, as what I've provided in this book is just the tip of the iceberg. You can go deeper into any of the chapters (in terms of research) discussed in the book to discover more and learn more about this great world of Hinduism.

The essence of Hinduism is the same essence of all true religions: Bhakti or pure love for God and genuine compassion for all beings. Radhanath Swami

Printed in the USA
CPSIA information can be obtained
at www.ICGtesting.com
LVHW011940021123
762861LV00034B/10

9 781952 191688